MAR

The
2023 Long Weekend Guide

James Cubby

NO BUSINESS HAS PAID A SINGLE PENNY OR GIVEN *ANYTHING*
TO BE INCLUDED IN THIS BOOK.

Fisher Collins Press

Copyright © - Fisher Collins Press
All rights reserved.

MARSEILLE
The Cubby
Long Weekend Guide

TABLE OF CONTENTS

Chapter 1 – WHY MARSEILLE? – 4

Chapter 2 – GETTING ABOUT – 10

Chapter 3 – WHERE TO STAY – 12
High on the Hog – Sensible Alternatives – On a Budget

Chapter 4 – WHERE TO EAT – 25
Ridiculously Extravagant – Moderate - Budget

Chapter 5 – NIGHTLIFE – 49

Chapter 6 – WHAT TO SEE & DO – 52

Chapter 7 – SHOPPING & SERVICES – 60

INDEX – 66

Chapter 1
WHY MARSEILLE?

It's so hard to begin when it comes to listing the great attributes of this truly unique city on the sea.

It's the oldest city in France, settled in ancient times by the Greeks. Marseille was already 500 years old when Caesar appeared at the city walls to lay siege in 49 B.C.

More recently, in the 20th Century, when immigrants from Algeria and other colonials from the remnant of the French Empire overseas started to swarm here, the city became quite unique in France because it was so culturally, psychologically and ethnically different from the rest of the country. Crime also soared as the city took on an image of grittiness and danger. But for all its ups and downs—and it's had plenty of both—Marseille has nonetheless remained a world-class city.

And while it's the biggest port in France (and the fifth largest in Europe), you still can see fishermen bring in their daily catch, an image that's as profound as any in all of Provence. The subtext to this amazing juxtaposition of old and new: It's all about the food.

The French national anthem, La Marseillaise, which we all remember from the movie "Casablanca," was written and composed by Claude Joseph Rouget de Lisle in 1792. The French National Convention adopted it as the Republic's anthem in 1795. The name of the song comes from the fact that it was first sung on the streets by volunteers from Marseille.

Because of its location, Marseille has for thousands of years been a crossroads where cultures combine (sometimes the word "combust" would seem more appropriate). This has given Marseille over the years a justified reputation for rough edges, for danger, for colorful characters, for a heady mix of internationalism, for crime. Many French themselves steer away from the teeming city, preferring the more sedate environs of nearby Avignon, Arles, Nîmes or Aix-en-Provence, none of them approaching the level of excitement or cosmopolitanism you get here in Marseille.

If you want to read a couple of excellent books around Marseille, read **M.F.K. Fisher's** "Consider the Oyster" or "The Gastronomical Me," when she, a naïve California girl, moved with her husband to Dijon before World War II. I love all her books. She captures the scruffiness of Marseille, the edginess of it, the *danger* of it.

When the European Union named Marseille a European Capital of Culture in 2013, an intense light shone on Marseille, giving it a more visible profile. And yes, the city has spruced itself up, added a new wardrobe, invigorated numerous new cultural institutions, opened new attractions, rehabbed hundreds of old warehouses into arts centers.

By the 12th Century Fort St.-Jean you'll cross a little bridge that leads you into the historic district of **Le Panier** (which translates as "the Basket"). This is where immigrants have long settled when they moved into Marseille from Italy or Corsica or Sicily or Turkey. Now it's home to an increasing number of artists. It's very hilly and made a perfect place for Resistance fighters to hide during World War II, so much so that the Nazis blew up parts of it.

The **Vieille Charité** is the center of the historic district. Here you'll find museums dedicated to exhibits of Mediterranean archaeology and African, Oceanic and American Indian art. The only way to absorb this part of town is to walk through it—through the narrowest streets and alleys lined on one side and the other with cafes, stores, workshops, artists' havens, fashionable lofts where you'd like to move tomorrow. The **Place des Moulins** at the top of the hill is where, shaded by trees, you'll find a square from which you can see miles out to sea. Artillery once stood here, forming a battery where they could shoot at approaching enemy ships.

If you go back down to Ft.-St. Jean, you'll see another bridge that leads you to a wide plaza, or esplanade, where the crowning jewel of Marseille's rebirth can be found, the new **Musée des Civilisations de l'Europe et de la Méditerranée** (**MuCEM**), designed by Rudy Ricciotti. (Interestingly, MuCEM is the first national museum ever designated outside Paris.) Also here is the Stefano Boeri-designed **Villa Méditerranée**. These two stunning museums were paid for with funds that came with the European Union designation. The money was well spent, let me tell you. From this vantage point you can see wide-ranging views of the city, all the way from the statue of **Notre-Dame de la Garde** on the south to the commanding **Cathédrale de la Major** on the north side.

It's well worth noting that the restaurants within MuCEM are run by **Chef Gerald Passédat,** who holds 3 Michelin stars.

Though these foods will be hard to avoid while visiting Marseille, I'm pointing them out here so that you know I want you to be certain to try them all because wherever in the world you travel, you won't get these dishes prepared any better than here in Marseille:

Aioli is a Provençal traditional sauce made of garlic, olive oil, lemon juice and egg yolks. There are many variations, but they're all good (to me, anyway). Just eat it with olives and you've got a treat.

Tapenade, a dish made of finely chopped or puréed olives, capers, anchovies and olive oil. Simply spread it on a crusty piece of bread and you're in heaven.

Bouillabaisse, that wonderful fresh fish soup from the sea, is so reminiscent of Marseille that I always think of the city whenever I order it elsewhere in the world. (And, like I said, it's almost never as good as they make it here.) Bouillabaisse has an interesting history. It originally was a stew made by Marseille fishermen using the bony rockfish restaurants and markets wouldn't buy from them. So they were stuck with it and had to make do. They tossed in vegetables, mussels, other shellfish, added different fish like bream, sea robin, monkfish, pretty much whatever was available. The result is a spectacularly flavorful stew you'll never forget (and find difficult to replicate).

Pastis. This is the drink of Provence. It's an anise-flavored liqueur and aperitif, usually 40% to 45% alcohol. I drink it day and night when I'm here. (It will kick your ass if you're not careful.)

After the important European Union designation, people have started to notice this city of less than 900,000. To see it in a new light, through a new perspective. And now they see what a truly fabulous place it is.

Funny thing, but Fisher knew it all those years ago when she swallowed the briny oysters she first found here, in wonderfully alive Marseille.

Chapter 2
GETTING ABOUT

The Public Transportation, also known as "**RTM**," offers a system of buses covering the city with 90 lines. The metro on the other hand has 2 lines only but 28 stops. The new tram system is a great service. You can count on making great use of it.

All services operate daily from 5 a.m. to 1 a.m. Cost is a couple of euros.

Check out the **City Pass** – this bargain allows you to get around the city cheaply. Information at the tourism site just below.

There is also a very convenient water shuttle from the Old Port.

The city offers a free bike service monitored with a tracking system from 6am to 12am daily with 130 stations.

TOURISM OFFICE OF MARSEILLE
11, la Canebière, (33-8) 26-50-05-00
www.marseille-tourisme.com

Chapter 3
WHERE TO STAY

AU VIEUX PANIER
13, rue du Panier, Marseille, 4-91-91-23-72
NEIGHBORHOOD: Hotel de Ville, Les Grandes Carmes
www.auvieuxpanier.com
This is a most unusual B&B in that it started out as a 17th Century Corsican grocer's shop. The 5 rooms were all decorated (each quite differently) by local artists. One, by Julien Colombier, is dark and sexy. Another, by Thomas Canto, is sleek and modern.

One has slabs of wood hanging from the ceiling. The public areas exhibit even more art on a rotating basis. In the middle of the historic old town.

BASTIDE DE CAPELONGUE
Les Claparèdes, Chemin des Cabanes, Bonnieux, +33 4 90 75 89 78
https://capelongue.com/?lang=en
NEIGHBORHOOD: Luberon.
Located in a rustic stone building, this upscale hotel offers 17 beautiful rooms – each carrying the name of a famous character from literature of Provence. Amenities include Free Wi-Fi, flat-screen TVs, and balconies (in some of the rooms). Facilities include: 2 restaurants with patio dining, an outdoor pool, gardens with sitting areas and a playground.

C2 HOTEL
48 Rue Roux de Brignoles, Marseille, +33 4 95 05 13 13
www.c2-hotel.com
NEIGHBORHOOD: Palais de Justice area
One thing you could never find in Marseille was the kind of "boutique" hotel you could find in almost any city anywhere. That has changed recently, like the C2 for example. Formerly a private 19th century mansion, this hotel features 20 spacious rooms. Amenities include free Wi-Fi and flat-screen TVs. Hotel features include spa with indoor pool and Jacuzzi, a bar, and a beach. You get to the beach by taking a 15-minute boat ride to their little island, Ile Degaby. Non-smoking hotel.

CASA HONORE
121, rue Sainte, Marseille, 33-4-91-33-08-34
NEIGHBORHOOD: Saint Victor
www.honoredeco.com/
This B&B was a printing plant before it was converted into 4 lovely rooms. They are small, but clean and modern. Marseille has 300 days of sunshine each year, and all that suns keeps the courtyard with its nice landscaping lush all year. Breakfast served in morning from 7. The lobby has cushy white seats and a huge wooden coffee table overlooking the yard, where there's also a swimming pool. Very cozy.

CHATEAU SAINT-MARTIN & SPA
2490 Avenue des Templiers, Vence, +33 4 93 58 02 02
www.chateau-st-martin.com
NEIGHBORHOOD: Vence
This luxury seasonal hotel offers plush rooms and beautiful views. If you enjoy sumptuous

appointments, you'll love the gilt-edged mirrors, parquet floors and tapestries you'll find when you walk into this place. Amenities include Free Wi-Fi and flat-screen TVs. Hotel features include marble bathrooms, balconies and terraces, an oak-paneled bar, a fine-dining restaurant, an outdoor grill, a spa, a pool, tennis courts, and access to a private beach.

HOTEL CRILLON LE BRAVE
Place de l'Eglise, Crillon-le-Brave, +33 4 90 65 61 61
www.crillonlebrave.com
NEIGHBORHOOD: Provence
This hotel includes several 17th & 18th century buildings with 28 double bedrooms in several sizes and 7 suites. Amenities include free Wi-Fi, CD & DVD library, mini-bar and safe, DVD and flat screen satellite TVs. Facilities include Pool, restaurant, bar, lounge and spa. Pet Friendly. Non-smoking rooms available.

HOTEL LA RESIDENCE
18, Quai du Port, Marseille, 4-91-91-91-22
NEIGHBORHOOD: Hotel de Ville
www.hotel-residence-marseille.com
Has commanding view of the harbor. Be sure to get a room with one of these great views. (Most rooms have this view, but make sure.) It'll be a big memory of your trip. This 40-room property was recently redesigned in a style reminiscent of Le Corbusier, very 1950s retro chic. You'll love the juxtaposition of the modern whimsical interior design here in the Old Port.

INTERCONTINENTAL MARSEILLE HOTEL DIEU
1 Place Daviel, Marseilles, 4-13-42-42-42
www.intercontinental.com
It may say Intercontinental on the building, but what's interesting here is the building that it's located in. It's a majestic 18th Century structure protected by a historic designation. It overlooks the Old Port and thus offers a panoramic view from its wide terrace. Next to the oldest part of Marseille, known as the Panier. Has all the amenities you'd expect at an Intercontinental: business center, courier service, email & Internet, concierge, secretarial service, extensive fitness center with spectacular floor to ceiling windows. There's a **Spa by Clarins** offering an indoor pool, 2 saunas and a hammam, 6 treatment booths. Also on site are **Les Fenêtres**, a brasserie, and the more upmarket **L'Alcyone**. Both menus feature local favorites of Provence.

L'OUSTALET
1476 Chemin des Marres, Simiane-Collongue, +33 6 49 76 53 55
www.loustalet-des-marres.com/en
NEIGHBORHOOD: La Bouilladisse
Beautiful B&B with 3 charming guestrooms. Designed for the traveler seeking an intimate, relaxing experience. Amenities include Free Wi-Fi, free breakfast, flat-screen TVs with satellite channels and free parking on-site. Facilities include seating areas, table tennis, and seasonal outdoor pool. Pet-friendly.

LA MAISON DOMAINE DE BOURNISSAC
Montée d'Eyragues, Paluds de Noves, +33 4 90 90 25 25
www.lamaison-a-bournissac.com
NEIGHBORHOOD: Provence
Set in a 15th-century traditional farmhouse, this hotel offers 13 guestrooms and suites – all decorated differently. Amenities include Free Wi-Fi, satellite TV, and unique features like marble bathrooms and exposed-stone walls. On-site Mediterranean restaurant with a terrace offering beautiful mountain views, outdoor pool, and sunny terrace. Ideal for a relaxing getaway.

LE COUVENT
HOTEL DE VILLE
6 rue Fonderie Vieille, Marseille, +33 6 12 31 48 79
https://www.fonderievieille.com/
NEIGHBORHOOD: Frankrike

This restored 17th Century convent offers 9 luxury suites complete with kitchen, Wi-Fi, TVs, and all the essentials. A favorite for visiting actors and artists. Conveniently located behind the Old Port, alongside the Place de Lenche, near the Museum of La vieille Charité and the MUCEM. Non-smoking venue. Pets not allowed.

LE CORBUSIER
280, Blvd Michelet, Marseille, 3-4-91-16-78-00
NEIGHBORHOOD: Sainte Anne
www.hotellecorbusier.com
Well known property a little out of the center of things, and that's why people cherish it. Not to mention that it was designed by the famed architect. The rooms here are decorated in a very Spartan manner, but they are comfortable and each room has a private terrace.

LE PETIT NICE PASSEDAT
17, rue des Braves, Marseille, +33 4 91 59 25 92
NEIGHBORHOOD: Endoume
www.passedat.fr
One of Marseille's most exclusive hotels. It was made by combining 2 villas. It's run by Gérald Passédat, who took over from his dad, Jean-Paul, and whose grandmother was famous opera singer. Boasts 3 Michelin stars. You'll want to dine here even if you don't stay here. The rooms are over-the-top modern and very luxurious.

LES BORIES HOTEL & SPA
Route de Senanque, Gordes, +33 4 90 72 00 51
www.hotellesbories.com
NEIGHBORHOOD: Luberon
Set on 20 acres, this sophisticated spa hotel offers 34 beautifully decorated rooms and suites. Amenities include Free Wi-Fi, flat-screen TVs, and mini-bars. Hotel facilities include spa features a menu of treatments, sauna, gym, a French restaurant, beautiful gardens, tennis court, indoor and outdoor pool, and guest lounge with a bar.

MGALLERY GRAND HOTEL BEAUVAU
4, rue Beauvau, Marseilles, 4- 91-54-91-00
www.mgallery.com/Marseilles
This Hotel is part of the famous Group "Accor." A four star recently renovated. Cozy and very quiet. Right in the heart of the old town, the color scheme is consistent with the colors of Provence. The interior is designed along the lines of Louis Philippe and Napoleon III. Legendary writers and musicians have stayed in this charming hotel, people like George Sand, Lamartine and Mérimée to Frédéric Chopin and Paganini. The rue Beauvau where this hotel is situated, is one of the oldest streets in all Marseille, as busy today as it ever has been. Try to get a room overlooking the Old Port.

MAMA SHELTER MARSEILLE
64, rue de la Loubiere, Marseille, 4-84-35-20-00
www.mamashelter.com
NEIGHBORHOOD: Cours Julien; Notre-Dame-du-Mont

I don't know what it is, but the ubiquitous Philippe Starck seems to have the magic touch of turning whatever property he designs into a trendy spot from the very moment it opens. (I wonder if Ian Schrager, who gave him such a high-profile boost when he worked on Schrager's New York hotels and then the Delano in South Beach, gets a commission—he ought to, as he's made Starck very rich.) What Schrager did was create the kind of fashionable hotel property that brought locals into the hotel, not just visitors. Thus, you get a heady mix of great people from in and out of town. This place is no different. And it's not in the most visible of locations. Still, people flock here like bees to honey. The restaurant here, by Chef Alain Senderens, is also a hot hangout. (The hotel reasonably priced, believe it or not, and near 3 Metro stops.)

SOFITEL MARSEILLE VIEUX PORT
36, Blvd Charles Livon, Marseille, 4-91-15-59-00
NEIGHBORHOOD: Le Pharo
www.sofitel-marseille-vieuxport.com
Upmarket hotel with lots of luxury and superior views of the Old Port. The fancy bar here is very popular. They even give pets a water bowl, or, if you like, a meal prepared for the dogs.

VILLA MARIE JEANNE
4 Rue Chicot, Marseille, +33 4 91 85 51 31
www.villa-marie-jeanne.com
NEIGHBORHOOD: Saint Barnabé
An 18th century stone manor house transformed into a wonderful Bed & Breakfast that offers 3 charming rooms, and 2 apartments. **Locals visit for the lovely restaurant on-site** serving fresh Mediterranean fish

and the dish Marseille is so famous for, Bouillabaisse. Here you'll eat family style on benches, sharing a table perhaps with locals. On-site boutique selling products of the land like olive oil, black truffle, and Bottarga. Amenities: Free Wi-Fi but need to bring your own toiletries.

Chapter 4
WHERE TO EAT

ALCYONE
INTERCONTINENTAL HOTEL DIEU
1 Place Daviel, Marseille, +33 4 13 42 43 43
www.ihg.com/intercontinental/hotels/gb/en/marseille/mrsha/hoteldetail#eatanddrink
CUISINE: French
DRINKS: Full bar

SERVING: Lunch & Dinner; closed Sun
PRICE RANGE: $$$$
NEIGHBORHOOD: Minta Arah
Michelin Star awarded restaurant that offers an innovative menu of seasonal dishes. The bouillabaisse here is a lot lighter than some of those you'll find elsewhere in town. Excellent French food served with a lighter touch. On game nights when the Olympique de Marseille soccer team plays, they open the terrace where they have a fun raucous grill night.

ARROSOIR DAMES
57 boulevard des Dames, 13002 Marseille, +33 9 54 22 65 71
www.arrosoir-marseille.com/
CUISINE: French Fusion/Mediterranean/Organic
DRINKS: Wine and Beer
SERVING: Lunch – Mon - Fri
PRICE RANGE: $$$
NEIGHBORHOOD: Alpes-Côte d'Azur
Organic eatery/grocery offering French Fusion cuisine. All dishes created from local and organic products. Vegetable dishes, omelettes, fish, and wide selection of desserts. Daily specials. Grocery sells regional organic products. Outdoor seating.

ASHOKA
7 rue Fortia, 13001 Marseille, +33 4 91 33 18 80
www.restaurant-ashoka.com/
CUISINE: Indian, Barbecue
DRINKS: No Booze
SERVING: Lunch & Dinner

PRICE RANGE: $$
Authentic Indian fare served here. (Some say it's the best Indian Food in Marseille.)
They serve dishes like chicken tikka, tandoori prawns and vegetable pakora. Nice wine selection.
Vegetarian options available. English and French spoken.

BAR DE LA MARINE
15, Quai de Rive Neuve, Marseille, 4-91-54-95-42
CUISINE: French, Mediterranean
DRINKS: Full Bar
SERVING: Breakfast & Lunch
PRICE RANGE: $$
NEIGHBORHOOD: Saint Victor

This famous Marseille institution is a popular spot for breakfast and lunch. At night, however, it becomes a bar only, and it's just as much fun.

CHEZ EMILIO
70 avenue de Mazargues, 13008 Marseille, +33 4 91 32 67 76
No Website
CUISINE: Italian/Mediterranean
DRINKS: Full bar
SERVING: Lunch & Dinner
PRICE RANGE: $$$$
NEIGHBORHOOD: 8th Arrondissement
Cute little combo grocery/eatery serving Italian cuisine with a French influence. Small simple menu but the choices are primo. Favorites include Argentinian Steak and Burrata. Large portions. Products for sale include Tuscan wines and a variety of oils and vinegars. Note: no air-conditioning.

CHEZ FONFON
140, rue Vallon des Auffes, Marseille, 4-91-52-14-38
www.chezfonfon.com
CUISINE: Seafood
DRINKS: Full bar
SERVING: Lunch & Dinner
PRICE RANGE: $$$$
NEIGHBORHOOD: Endoume
Tucked away in a small inlet, Chez Fonfon has a wonderful view. In the summer, you can ride around the port in a boat. This is where you'll want to order the bouillabaisse. They're also famous for their roasted pigeon.

EPICERIE L'IDEAL
11 rue d'Aubagne, 13001 Marseille, +33 9 80 39 99 41
www.epicerielideal.com
CUISINE: French/Deli

DRINKS: Beer & Wine
SERVING: Breakfast, Lunch, & Dinner; closed Sun & Mon
PRICE RANGE: $$
NEIGHBORHOOD: Noailles
Grocery store that offers a simple menu that changes daily. You'll find French and Italian gourmet goods bulging from the wooden shelves lining the walls. A few tables are available where you can eat. Busy all day with a loyal following. Meals prepared with fresh seasonal products. Vegetarian options. Nice selection of beers.

KAHENA
2 rue de la Republique, 13001 Marseille, +33 4 91 90 61 93
www.lakahena.fr/
CUISINE: African/Mediterranean/Middle Eastern
DRINKS: Wine only
SERVING: Lunch & Dinner
PRICE RANGE: $$$
NEIGHBORHOOD: Near the Old Port
Authentic Tunisian eatery serving grilled meats and fishes, salads, and couscous. Couscous is their specialty offering 10 varieties. Finish your meal with one of their homemade cakes: Kataif, Baklava, Makroud, and Oriental pastries. Nice selection of wines.

L'EPUISETTE
Vallon des Auffes, Marseille, +33 4 91 52 17 82
www.l-epuisette.fr/
CUISINE: French/Mediterranean

DRINKS: Full bar
SERVING: Lunch & Dinner; closed Sun & Mon
PRICE RANGE: $$$$
NEIGHBORHOOD: Endoume

There's been some sort of eatery on this spot—a rocky promontory jutting out into the sea beside a charming little fishing village—for over 50 years. From this vantage point you can see the Chateau d'If, an island fortress dating back to the 16th Century. What started out as nothing more than a little seafood shack has transformed into a light, modern restaurant decorated with travertine marble and light-colored woods. Great menu of French cuisine – try the tasting menu if you've never been here. The authentic Bouillabaisse here is served in 2 courses. First you get a deep brown bouillon made using bony rockfish and spiced with garlic and saffron. Next you'll get fillets of 5 different fish (monkfish, scorpion fish, gurnard, weever, John Dory), first stewed and then sauced at your table with more bouillon. There's a great appetizer of tuna with foi gras that's quite different from any version I've seen before. Extensive wine list representing all parts of Europe.

LA BOITE A SARDINE
2 boulevard de la Liberation, 13001 Marseille
+33 4 91 50 95 95
www.laboiteasardine.com
CUISINE: Seafood
DRINKS: Wine & Beer

SERVING: Breakfast/Lunch/Early Dinner
PRICE RANGE: $$$
NEIGHBORHOOD: Thier
Tiny restaurant offering a great selection of fresh seafood including lobster, chilled shrimp, raw, freshly shucked oysters and sea urchins. Menu changes daily because they have no written menu, just what seafood they are serving that day. Reservations recommended otherwise you can wait up to an hour. Note: they only speak French here.

LA CANTINETTA
24, Cours Julien F, Marseille, 33-4-91-48-10-48
http://www.restaurantlacantinetta.fr/
CUISINE: Italian
DRINKS: Full Bar
SERVING: Lunch & Dinner
PRICE RANGE: $$
NEIGHBORHOOD: Notre Dame du Mont

No more French food for you? (If such a thing was possible.) Try this place for great Italian specialties. Big hams of prosciutto dangle from the ceiling. The mozzarella is made from cow's milk from Puglia. I always get the superbly grilled veal chop when stopping in here, and in good weather, I always sit in the very nice garden out back.

LA CARAVELLE
Hotel Belle Vue
34 quai du Port, Marseilles, +33 4 91 90 36 64
http://www.lacaravelle-marseille.com/
CUISINE: Provencal
DRINKS: Beer & Wine
SERVING: Breakfast, Lunch, & Dinner
PRICE RANGE: $$
NEIGHBORHOOD: Port
Located in the Hotel Belle Vue, this dark little restaurant and jazz venue has been open since the 1930s. Tables are close together, giving the place a cozy packed feeling. Lots of energy. Try to get a table

by the narrow windows and you'll get a great view of the old port. Or, when the weather's nice, sit outside. They have some tables out on the terrace overlooking the water. Menu out front is in French, but the staff will help translate. Favorites: Swordfish; Sardines; Smoked Lamb. Nice wine list.

LA FONTAINE CASTELLANE
31 avenue Jules Cantini, 13006 Marseille, +33 4 91 79 05 02
No Website
CUISINE: African/Moroccan/Mediterranean
DRINKS: No Booze
SERVING: Lunch & Dinner; Sunday Brunch only
PRICE RANGE: $
NEIGHBORHOOD: 6th Arrondissement
Known for their authentic couscous, this Moroccan/Tunisian eatery also serves brick, samosa-like wraps, fish and lamb dishes. Generous portions. Nice selection of pastries. French & English spoken.

LA NAUTIQUE
20 quai de Rive Neuve, Marseilles, +33 4 91 33 01 78
http://www.restaurantlanautique.fr/
CUISINE: French/Seafood/Mediterranean
DRINKS: Full Bar
SERVING: Lunch, Dinner
PRICE RANGE: $$
NEIGHBORHOOD: Port
Located on a floating pavilion that juts out into the marina where the boats bobbing about on three sides give you a spectacular view of marina activity. La

Nautique is quite an institution. Menu of traditional French/Mediterranean cuisine.

LE BOUCHER
10 Rue de Village, 13006 Marseille, +33 4 91 48 79 65
No Website
CUISINE: Steakhouse/French
DRINKS: Full bar
SERVING: Lunch & Dinner; closed Sun & Mon
PRICE RANGE: $$$
NEIGHBORHOOD: Castellane
Friendly steakhouse offering a simple menu with a French twist offering a variety of beef dishes but also European favorites like pig feet and lamb sweetbreads. Ideal for meat lovers. Nice wine selection. Reservations recommended.

LE MOLE PASSÉDAT
Prom. Pierre Laffont, Marseille, +33 4 91 19 17 80
www.passedat.fr/en
CUISINE: French/Mediterranean fusion
DRINKS: Full bar
SERVING: Lunch & Dinner; closed Sun
PRICE RANGE: $$$
NEIGHBORHOOD: La Joliette
This super chic modern restaurant is located on the top floor of the MUCEM museum where you'll really love the expansive terrace offering a great view. In fact, the view is probably the best one in the whole town—it overlooks the old port, the hills on top of which are perched ancient churches, and of course the

Mediterranean Sea. There are choices here—a buffet on the terrace loaded with charcuterie items and great salads, seafood and cocktails. The other one is **La Table**, a much more upscale dining experience that requires reservations. Creative menu of dishes like: Octopus carpaccio; spelt risotto; pan-fried duck's liver; and crab meat with a lemony quinoa salad. The wine list emphasizes wines from Provence, as it should.

LE PATIO DU PRADO
9 Rue Borde, Marseilles, +33 4 91 40 61 43
http://www.le-patio-du-prado-restaurant-marseille.com/ WEBSITE DOWN AT PRESSTIME
CUISINE: French
DRINKS: Beer & Wine
SERVING: Lunch &Dinner, Dinner only on Saturdays, Closed Sundays
PRICE RANGE: $$
NEIGHBORHOOD: Le Rouet
This small eatery couldn't get more charming if it tried—has two levels inside and some patio seating on the first level. Has a simple menu of French cuisine. Seafood and pizzas. Daily blackboard specials, and I always choose something from this short list. Nice selection of wines.

LE PETIT NICE PASSEDAT
17, rue des Braves, Marseille, 4-91-59-25-92
www.passedat.fr
CUISINE: French, Southwest
DRINKS: Full Bar
SERVING: Lunch & Dinner
PRICE RANGE: $$$$
NEIGHBORHOOD: Endoume
This expensive eatery is the city's only restaurant with 3 Michelin stars. Here, you'll want to focus on the fish, fish, fish. Take the #83 bus from the Old Port and disembark at Anse de la Fausse Monnaie. Go down to the harbor and you'll be there. Well worth the high prices.

LE VENTRE DE L'ARCHITECTE
280, Blvd Michelet, Marseille, 4-9-16-78-23
www.hotellecorbusier.com/restaurant/
CUISINE: French
DRINKS: Full Bar
SERVING: Lunch & Dinner
PRICE RANGE: $$$$
NEIGHBORHOOD: Bompard
There are some Asian influences in this cuisine. Very expensive, but it's quite a show. (The views are excellent.)

LES ARCENAULX
25, cours Honoré d'Estienne d'Orves, Marseilles, 4-91-59-80-30
www.les-arcenaulx.com
CUISINE: French, Regional
DRINKS: Full Bar
SERVING: Lunch & Dinner
PRICE RANGE: $$$$
This is a 30-year-old landmark. While the walls are lined with books like a library, you won't want to bury your nose in a book while you're here. You can expect a delectable culinary experience such as the scallops on a bed of sweet potato galette. Refined cuisine in a pleasant atmosphere. Enjoy the desserts as well with a great selection of teas in the afternoon. Excellent service.

MIRAMAR
12, quai du Port, Marseilles, 4-91-91-10-40
www.lemiramar.fr
CUISINE: French, Regional Southwestern
DRINKS: Full Bar
SERVING: Lunch & Dinner
PRICE RANGE: $$$$
The concierge at my hotel gave me several recommendations for dining. This was one of them and I wasn't disappointed. The Bouillabaisse here is for two persons, delivered tableside, beautifully presented. Infused with "Ricard." It has a distinctive flavor. Incredible fish soup. Very pricey but the quality is all here.

MONTREAL CAFÉ
4 rue Saint Thome, 13002 Marseille, +33 4 26 85 36 23
www.montrealcafe.fr
CUISINE: American, Vegetarian Friendly
DRINKS: Full Bar
SERVING: Lunch Fri-Mon, Breakfast on Mondays.
PRICE RANGE: $
NEIGHBORHOOD: Panier
Freshly made bagels are the specialty here. Great choice for American breakfast dishes or bagel sandwiches. Everything here is freshly made. Friendly staff that speaks English and French. Outdoor seating.

PÉRON
56 Promenade de la Corniche John Kennedy, Marseille, +33 4 91 52 15 22
www.restaurant-peron.com
CUISINE: Modern European/Seafood
DRINKS: Full bar
SERVING: Lunch & Dinner
PRICE RANGE: $$$$
NEIGHBORHOOD: Endoume
Great upscale French eatery (food is as good as that at Le Petit Nice, but not as expensive) that fills up with locals – first seating at 8 p.m. is recommended before it gets busy. Expect a traditional 7 course French dinner. Extensive wine list. Great views overlooking the Mediterranean Sea. Delicious desserts – order early as they run out.

QUESARITO
131 Bd de la Libération, 13001 Marseille, +33 7 82 81 29 23
https://quesarito.fr/
CUISINE: Mexican
DRINKS: No Booze
SERVING: Lunch & Dinner, closed Tuesdays

PRICE RANGE: $
NEIGHBORHOOD: Saint Charles
Mexican eatery Chipotle-style. Nice stop for lunch. Typical Mexican fast-food fare like guacamole, quesadillas, and tacos. Vegetarian options. Try the Jarritos (fruit flavored drinks). French and English spoken here.

SOUS LES MICOCOULIERS
13810 Traverse Montfort, Eygalières, +04 90 95 94 53
https://lemicoc.com/
CUISINE: French/Provencal
DRINKS: Full bar
SERVING: Lunch & Dinner
PRICE RANGE: $$$
NEIGHBORHOOD: Traverse Montfort
Chef Pierre Louis Poize offers a gourmet menu focusing on local and seasonal ingredients. The restaurant features indoor and outdoor dining – check out the beautiful courtyard with 200-year-old trees. Menu picks: Lobster grilled with chestnuts and Carpachio Salmon. Nice wine list.

SUMO SUSHI BAR
120 rue Condorcet Entry Andre Roussin Boulevard, 13016 Marseille, +33 4 91 42 11 27
https://mysumo.fr/
CUISINE: Japanese/Sushi
DRINKS: Full bar
SERVING: Breakfast & Lunch, Mon - Fri
PRICE RANGE: $$$

NEIGHBORHOOD: Near Bank Populaire
Located on the outskirts of Marseille, this little unpretentious eatery serves sushi made from fresh, locally sourced produce. Japanese specialties served like Maki, Nigiri and Sashimi and Chirashi. Delicious Miso and Yakitori soups. Weekly specials. Vegetarian options. Impressive selection of desserts – try their Tiramisu.

VILLA MARIE JEANNE
4 Rue Chicot, Marseille, +33 4 91 85 51 31
www.villa-marie-jeanne.com
NEIGHBORHOOD: Saint Barnabé
An 18th century stone manor house transformed into a wonderful Bed & Breakfast that offers 3 charming rooms, and 2 apartments. **Locals visit for the lovely**

restaurant on-site serving fresh Mediterranean fish and the dish Marseille is so famous for, Bouillabaisse. Here you'll eat family style on benches, sharing a table perhaps with locals. On-site boutique selling products of the land like olive oil, black truffle, and Bottarga. Amenities: Free Wi-Fi but need to bring your own toiletries.

BISTRO MIMI
(formerly VINONÉO)
6 place Daviel, Marseilles, +33 4 88 86 15 27
https://www.bistrot-mimi-restaurant-marseille.com/
CUISINE: French/Mediterranean
DRINKS: Full Bar
SERVING: Lunch, Dinner
PRICE RANGE: $$
NEIGHBORHOOD: Le Panier
Sit outside in the shadow of an old church, or inside where the modern décor clashes (not unpleasantly) with the ancient building where the place is housed.

Known for their wines, this family restaurant offers a variety of homemade dishes (even the ice cream is made here). The presentation is expert and the dishes look great when placed before you. Favorites: Salmon tartare and Pork ribs. Creative desserts like Peach crumble with mango ice cream. Vegetarian friendly.

Chapter 5
NIGHTLIFE

Marseille's best nightlife can be found on rooftops and open-air venues.

AU PETIT NICE
28, Place Jean Jaures, Marseille, 4-91-48-43-04
NEIGHBORHOOD: Le Camas; La Plaine
No Website
Nice bar in trendy La Plaine.

LA CARAVELLE
34 Quai du Port, 13002 Marseille, +33 4 91 90 36 64
www.lacaravelle-marseille.com/bar/
NEIGHBORHOOD: Hotel de Ville
Old-school bistro around since the 1930s. Tiny terrace on the second floor offers views of the Old Port. Small menu of tapas and bar snacks. Impressive selection of wines and cocktails. Closes 12:30 a.m.

LE BAR DE LA MARINE
15 Quai de Rive Neuve, 13007 Marseille, +33 4 91 54 95 42
NEIGHBORHOOD: Saint Victor
One of the most famous bars in the city as it has served as a backdrop/location for many French films of the 1930s. Great place for lunch or a cocktail on

the terrace facing the Old Port. Nice selection of international beers. Open until midnight.

LE CARRE
36, Blvd Charles Livon, Marseille, 4-91-15-59-60
NEIGHBORHOOD: Le Pharo
www.sofitel-marseille-vieuxport.com
Here in the lobby of the **Sofitel Vieux Port** is a lovely lounge with lots of specialty cocktails to go with the killer view of the Vieux Port.

LA PART DES ANGES
33 Rue Sainte, 13001 Marseille, +33 4 91 33 55 70
NEIGHBORHOOD: Opéra
Funky local wine shop/bar with a simple menu. Friendly hangout to have a glass or bottle of wine. Simple bar menu. Closes 2 a.m.

L'UNIC
11 Cr Jean Ballard, 13001 Marseille, +33 4 91 33 45 84
NEIGHBORHOOD: Opéra
Nice little corner bar with a nice selection of cocktails, whiskeys, and beers (local and international). Open late night. Crowd changes from an older crowd to a younger group later in the evening.

Chapter 6
WHAT TO SEE & DO

CENTRE DE LA VIEILLE CHARITE
2, rue de la Charite, Marseille, 4-91-14-58-80
NEIGHBORHOOD: Les Grandes Carmes
www.vieille-charite-marseille.com/
This used to be an almshouse, but it has been creatively turned into a great museum, or really, a series of museums and arts institutions. In 1640, following the royal edict on "confinement of the poor and beggars," the City of Marseille, the owner of land located on the northern slope of the hills, decided to

build the Old Charity to accommodate the beggars. But the project stalled and it was only in 1670 that Pierre Puget, the king's architect who was from the area, began one of his greatest achievements. It's been going ever since. This charming neighborhood makes for a good stroll. What used to be a home for sailors, immigrants and the poor, with its cobbled streets and colorfully painted houses, now is home to artisans and professional people.

CROISIERES MARSEILLE CALANQUES
1 Canebière, Marseille, 4-91-58-50-58
NEIGHBORHOOD: Opera
www.croisieres-marseille-calanques.com
A variety of tours available here. Don't forget that Marseille was settled by the Greeks around 600 BC. To get a good idea what the sometimes-unforgiving rugged coast looks like, take one of these cheap hour-long boat tours. You'll want to see the "Calanques,"

the series of stunning limestone cliffs and coves stretching between Marseille and Cassis. (These were recently named the newest national park in France.) On either side of the port, you'll see from the water the 2 forts dating back to the 17th Century: St.-Jean (goes back to the 12th Century) and St.-Nicolas. Another treat is the **Cathédrale de la Major**, designed in the Byzantine style, as well as the **Île d'If** and its fort, the **Château d'If**. This 16th Century fortress was later turned into a prison made famous by Dumas in "**The Count of Monte Cristo.**"

LA BASTIDE DES BAINS
19, rue Sainte, Marseille, 4-91-33-39-13
NEIGHBORHOOD: Opera
www.bastide-des-bains.com
Traditional hammam (Turkish bath) housed in an old printing house.

LA CORNICHE
This is the famous boulevard that hugs the Mediterranean that you'll want to walk up and down as you take in the sights and inhale the salty air.

LA S JULIEN
Cours Julien, Marseille, No Phone
NEIGHBORHOOD: Notre Dame du Mont
Scenic courtyard that attracts the young and hip. Lots of places to hang out, with bars and cafes and boutiques everywhere.

LE PALAIS DU PHARO
58, Blvd Charles Livon, Marseille, 4-91-14-64-95
NEIGHBORHOOD: Le Pharo
http://palaisdupharo.marseille.fr
You can sit on the lawn at **Napoleon III's Palace** by the sea to look at the great view and the other people looking at it with you.

MUSEE D'ART CONTEMPORAIN MAC
69, Ave de Haifa, Marseille, +33 4 13 94 83 50
https://musees.marseille.fr/
NEIGHBORHOOD: Sainte Anne
The late César Baldaccini was the most renowned of local arts champions. This museum is crammed with his neo-realist sculptures. Like the compacted autos that always attract curious stares. Many other artists represented, such as Jean-Michel Basquiat and Dieter Roth.

MuCEM
MUSÉE DES CIVILISATIONS DE L'EUROPE ET DE LA MÉDITERRANÉE
MUSEUM OF EUROPEAN & MEDITERRANEAN CIVILIZATIONS
+33 4 84 35 13 13
www.mucem.org/
Right on the edge of the port of Marseille is this spectacular museum that opened in 2016. Not only

does it have stunning views of the harbor and the sea, but the architecture is eye opening as well. Its

historical collections are superior and their exhibitions cover not only European but North African cultures as well, recognizing the importance over the centuries that Africa has played in the growth and development of Marseille. The job of putting this all together fell to architect Rudy Ricciotti, who worked hard to combine the new building with the 17th Century Fort St.-Jean, connecting it using foot bridges to the modernist glass structure. The outdoor skin covering the top of the building represents a fishing net, so perfect for Marseille, right?

NOTRE-DAME-DU-MONT
This neighborhood is close to three metro stations. It is a short walk to the Old Port, popular for its bars and restaurants and for the Notre-Dame Church atop a hill that towers above it all.

Chapter 7
SHOPPING & SERVICES

You will want to check out the **Cours Julien** district—this is where you'll find lots of interesting shops.

AMERICAN VINTAGE
31 Rue Francis Davso, Marseille, 4-91-33-43-46
www.americanvintage-store.com/fr
An empty suitcase could be useful as you hit Rue Sainte, where local fashion labels have sprouted up. Though the name is misleading — the brand is Marseille-based and sells new threads — the subdued colors and ultrathin fabrics have garnered enough

fans to generate boutiques from Amsterdam to Tel Aviv.

COMPAGNIE DE PROVENCE
18, rue Davso, 33-4-91-33-04-17
1, rue Crates, Marseille, 4-91-56-20-94
www.compagniedeprovence.com
Olive and vegetable-based soaps. They have 2 shops here in town. I once got some lavender scented exfoliating soap in this shop and use it to this day. (I still order from them, only now I do it through Amazon.) Really great soaps.

LES DOCKS
10 Place de la Joliette, Marseille, +33 4 91 44 25 28
http://www.lesdocks-marseille.com/en/
NEIGHBORHOOD: La Joliette
This unique complex is a recently opened city center that houses over 200 companies, situated in a series of cargo warehouses and terminals that make the port even more pedestrian friendly than it was before.

Approximately 60 shopping outlets, local restaurants, service providers and artisans. Open daily.

LES HALLES DE LA MAJOR
Les Voûtes de la Major, 12 Quai de la Tourette, Marseille, +33 4 91 45 80 10
www.leshallesdelamajor.com/en/
NEIGHBORHOOD: **La Joliette**
By day a farmer's market and food hall featuring great selections of gourmet foods, sandwiches, seafood, and local cuisine. Open seating at picnic tables, ultra-casual. A great selection of different foods—try to veal tartare at **La Boucherie**, or the excellent mint fritters or the delectable fried zucchini rom **Las Tapas des Halles**. From **La Poissonnerie**, you can refresh yourself with a plate for salty oysters. At night the place is transformed into a gathering place and venue for special events and entertainment.

SESSUN
6, rue Sainte, Marseilles, 4-91-52-33-61
NEIGHBORHOOD: Vauban
www.sessun.com
The colors and design get more adventurous at, where you can pick up funky hot pants with a graph-paper motif.

ZEIN ORIENTAL SPA
16, Quai Rive Neuve, Marseille, 4-91-59-11-11
https://marseille.zeinorientalspa.fr
NEIGHBORHOOD: Saint Victor
Tucked in an alley along the Vieux Port, an upscale hammam-spa that opened last year, is very 1,001 Nights with its keyhole doorways, Moorish tilework, spice-scented air and soft Arabo-electro music. The Hammam Jasmin package includes a rubdown in olive-oil soap, an exfoliation by an attendant with a rough glove, and a half-hour massage.

INDEX

A

African, 30, 35
Aioli, 8
ALCYONE, 25
American, 42
ARROSOIR DAMES, 26
ASHOKA, 26
AU PETIT NICE, 49

AU VIEUX PANIER, 12

B

BAR DE LA MARINE, 27
Barbecue, 26
BASTIDE DE CAPELONGUE, 13
Bouillabaisse, 8

C

C2 HOTEL, 13
CASA HONORE, 14
Cathédrale de la Major, 7, 54
CENTRE DE LA VIEILLE CHARITE, 52
Château d'If, 54
CHATEAU SAINT-MARTIN & SPA, 14
CHEZ EMILIO, 28
CHEZ FONFON, 29
City Pass, 10
COMPAGNIE DE PROVENCE, 61
Cours Julien, 60
CROISIERES MARSEILLE CALANQUES, 53

E

EPICERIE L'IDEAL, 29

F

French, 25, 30, 36, 44
French Fusion, 26

H

Hotel Belle Vue, 34
HOTEL CRILLON LE BRAVE, 15
HOTEL DE VILLE, 18
HOTEL LA RESIDENCE, 16

I

Île d'If, 54

Indian, 26
INTERCONTINENTAL HOTEL DIEU, 25
INTERCONTINENTAL MARSEILLE HOTEL DIEU, 17
Italian, 28

J

Japanese, 44

K

KAHENA, 30

L

L'Alcyone, 17
L'EPUISETTE, 30
L'OUSTALET, 18
L'UNIC, 51
LA BASTIDE DES BAINS, 54
LA BOITE A SARDINE, 32
La Boucherie, 62
LA CANTINETTA, 33
LA CARAVELLE, 34, 50
LA CORNICHE, 55
LA FONTAINE CASTELLANE, 35
LA MAISON DOMAINE DE BOURNISSAC, 18
LA NAUTIQUE, 35
LA PART DES ANGES, 51
La Poissonnerie, 62
La Table, 37
Las Tapas des Halles, 62
LE BAR DE LA MARINE, 50
LE BOUCHER, 36
LE CARRE, 51
LE CORBUSIER, 19

LE COURS JULIEN, 55
LE COUVENT, 18
LE MOLE PASSEDAT, 36
LE PALAIS DU PHARO, 55
Le Panier, 6
LE PATIO DU PRADO, 37
LE PETIT NICE PASSEDAT, 19, 38
LE VENTRE DE L'ARCHITECTE, 39
LES ARCENAULX, 40
LES BORIES HOTEL & SPA, 20
LES DOCKS, 61
Les Fenêtres, 17
LES HALLES DE LA MAJOR, 62

M

MAMA SHELTER MARSEILLE, 21
Mediterranean, 26, 30, 36
Mexican, 43
MGALLERY BEAUVAU HOTEL, 20
Middle Eastern, 30
MIRAMAR, 41
Modern European, 43
MONTREAL CAFÉ, 42
Moroccan, 35
MuCEM, 7, 56
MUSEE D'ART CONTEMPORAIN MAC, 56
Musée des Civilisations de l'Europe et de la Méditerranée, 7
MUSÉE DES CIVILISATIONS DE L'EUROPE ET DE LA MÉDITERRANÉE, 56

MUSEUM OF EUROPEAN & MEDITERRANEAN CIVILIZATIONS, 56

N

Napoleon III's Palace, 55
Notre-Dame de la Garde, 7
NOTRE-DAME-DU-MONT, 58

O

Organic, 26

P

Pastis, 9
PÉRON, 43
Place des Moulins, 6
Provencal, 44

Q

QUESARITO, 43

R

RTM, 10

S

Seafood, 43
SESSUN, 63
SOFITEL MARSEILLE VIEUX PORT, 22
SOUS LES MICOCOULIERS, 44
Spa by Clarins, 17

Steakhouse, 36
SUMO SUSHI BAR, 44

T

Tapenade, 8
The Count of Monte Cristo.", 54
TOURISM OFFICE OF MARSEILLE, 11

V

Vieille Charité, 6
VILLA MARIE JEANNE, 22, 45
Villa Méditerranée, 7
VINONÉO, 46

Z

ZEIN ORIENTAL SPA, 64

Ingram Content Group UK Ltd.
Milton Keynes UK
UKHW021256280423
420941UK00024B/579